First Responders

Community Colleges on the Front Line of Security

American Association of Community Colleges
Underwritten by the AT&T Foundation

The American Association of Community Colleges (AACC) is the primary advocacy organization for the nation's community colleges. The association represents more than 1,100 two-year, associate degree–granting institutions and more than 11 million students. AACC promotes community colleges through six strategic action areas: national and international recognition and advocacy, learning and accountability, leadership development, economic and workforce development, connectedness across AACC membership, and international and intercultural education. Information about AACC and community colleges may be found at www.aacc.nche.edu.

American Association of Community Colleges
One Dupont Circle, NW
Suite 410
Washington, DC 20036

Printed in the United States of America.

Contents

Preface

As the largest sector of higher education, community colleges play a unique role in ensuring access to quality postsecondary education and specialized training programs to almost half (45%) of all U.S. undergraduates. What is less widely recognized is the critical involvement the colleges have in the preparation of the nation's first responders—professionals such as law enforcement officers, firefighters, emergency medical technicians, and others who are typically first on the scene in the event of trauma or disaster.

The events and images of September 11, 2001, seared into our national psyche the importance such professionals play in protecting our communities and our citizenry. Homeland security became the obsession of a generation, and policymakers began to redefine what was needed to protect our nation. Community colleges responded to this compelling need, reaching out to help with local and regional preparedness planning, integrating new elements into existing education and training programs or establishing new ones, offering to share facilities and resources, and even developing or adapting highly specialized facilities and equipment.

To gain a more complete picture of community college involvement in homeland security efforts, the American Association of Community Colleges (AACC) undertook two important surveys in 2004. Findings from these studies—AACC's Hot Programs and Homeland Security Survey and Survey on Homeland Security and Related Issues—provided for the first time an in-depth look at these broad and varied activities and provided the basis for much of this report, *First Responders: Community Colleges on the Front Line of Homeland Security.*

Conducted during the spring of 2004, AACC's Hot Programs and Homeland Security Survey asked community college chief academic officers to identify those programs for which there was a large market demand for their graduates. Not surprisingly, nursing, law enforcement, and allied health occupations consistently ranked as top hot programs nationally, reflecting the tremendous need for more of these skilled professionals. More surprising was how many respondents reported that they had reviewed or modified their curricula to address increased homeland security needs.

As the Bush Administration was developing its homeland security strategies and programs, AACC wanted to ensure that community colleges were recognized as part of the critical U.S. infrastructure network and as a key asset in states and localities. It also wanted community colleges to be in a better position to influence federal policy and programmatic decisions for federal appropriations related to homeland security training initiatives. Thus, in November 2003, AACC's Board of Directors moved to create an Ad Hoc Task Force on Homeland Security to help AACC develop both short- and long-term strategies in the homeland security area. The task force would serve as a resource for the board and make specific recommendations on AACC's positions in the area of homeland security and public safety.

At the urging of AACC's Ad Hoc Task Force on Homeland Security, AACC launched a second more comprehensive survey of community college homeland security and related programs and facilities. During the summer of 2004, community college presidents and chancellors were asked to indicate on a Web-based survey in which disciplines their institutions offered programs or courses as well as what specialized facilities or partnerships their colleges offered to support homeland security efforts. As you will discover in this report, an astonishing number of community colleges offer degree and certificate programs for first responders—law enforcement officers, firefighters, and emergency medical technicians—as well as myriad other important programs for nurses, allied health professionals, utility workers, and more.

This report would not have been possible without the detailed information provided by the 760 community college CEOs who responded to the 2004 AACC

Survey on Homeland Security and Related Issues and the hundreds of community college chief academic officers that responded to AACC's 2004 Hot Programs and Homeland Security Survey.

Special thanks are due to the AACC Ad Hoc Task Force members for their help in drafting the initial survey instrument and to the AACC staff and SRI International research team members who perfected the survey design and compiled the survey data.

AACC is grateful to the AT&T Foundation for underwriting the development of this groundbreaking report.

George R. Boggs
President and CEO
American Association of Community Colleges

Executive Summary

Community colleges are, by tradition and mission, reflective of and responsive to the communities they serve. Thus, when the events of September 11, 2001, made ensuring the security of our communities and the nation a more urgent concern, the question became not if, but how and how broadly, community colleges would become engaged to meet this new and compelling need. As the nation stepped up its efforts to identify threats and work to preempt catastrophes or deal with them expeditiously, the critical need for trained personnel, resources, and facilities became clear. The devastation to the Gulf Coast region caused by the 2005 hurricanes would later underscore awareness that *homeland security* encompasses natural as well as human-made disasters and that localities, as well as the federal government, need planning, coordination, and professional response teams to deal with disasters.

But specifically how is the national network of more than 1,100 community colleges responding to homeland security needs, and how might the efforts of colleges that have made responding to those needs a priority serve as models for others? Answering the first question became the focus of a 2004 survey commissioned by the American Association of Community Colleges (AACC). (See www.aacc.nche.edu/HomelandSecurityReport.) Answering the second question is the purpose of this report, *First Responders: Community Colleges on the Front Line of Security.*

With an emphasis on partnerships and civic engagement, the report delineates three primary areas in which community colleges function as the front line for dealing with disasters: planning, education and training, and sharing resources and facilities. It is important to note that, even before September 11, 2001, when calls for coordinated homeland security efforts became more widespread and insistent, community colleges were already providing training, resources, and coordination for much locally based security work.

Responses to AACC's survey indicated that the majority of community colleges were actively engaged in training first and second responders. This finding is supported by data from the National Center for Education Statistics (2003), indicating that close to 80% of the nation's firefighters, police, and emergency medical technicians are credentialed by community colleges. In addition, because of their accessibility and culture of service, colleges function as community centers, used as sites for civic planning, as a catalyst and resource for economic development, and, in times of crisis, as community shelters and communications centers.

Thus, community colleges can rightly be viewed as natural partners of community, state, and federal governments when disaster strikes, and their responses to large disasters, such as the World Trade Center attacks and Hurricanes Katrina and Rita, as well as to smaller, localized ones, have validated that assertion. This report documents the range of functions and contributions community colleges are currently providing and serves as a guide to colleges who seek to expand their engagement in local and national security preparedness.

INVOLVEMENT IN PLANNING

The *community* nature of community colleges suggests that they are in and of their communities. Although when many community colleges were founded in the period between 1950 and 1975 that mission may have been limited to training students for their first jobs in the community, it rapidly evolved into economic development, community development, on-the-job training, transitional training, and recreational activities, so that, by the 1990s, community colleges were integral to community life and development on many levels. It was during that period, for example, that many localities shifted their first responder training to community colleges.

This pivotal position of the community college within the community allows it to take on new coordinating and planning goals related to homeland security, including the following:

- Coordinating with state and federal agencies to initiate and customize programs to meet broader community needs.
- Participating in national initiatives, such as the Federal Emergency Management Agency's Emergency Management Institute, thereby becoming part of a planning and training network that connects resources and training across the country.
- Leading or engaging in statewide initiatives and setting up regional consortia that serve the particular needs of their area.
- Leveraging their resources with other institutions to provide greater service than any one institution could provide.
- Forming partnerships that pool expertise and allow them to function as regional or national centers for training in specific homeland security areas.
- Initiating discussions and planning processes for new disaster management initiatives.

EDUCATING AND TRAINING HOMELAND SECURITY PROFESSIONALS

Already the primary providers of pre-service training for first responders and more than 60% of new nurses, community colleges expanded and refined their programs in the post–September 11, 2001, timeframe. Many colleges now offer cybersecurity options at degree and certificate levels. Many existing police and firefighter training programs now devote more time to dealing with terrorism, hazardous materials, and explosive devices. Airport security training has grown from a relatively small number of programs before 2001 to a larger number today. Several colleges are even exploring areas such as dealing with weapons of mass destruction, maritime security, and agro-terrorism, although those kinds of specializations tend to be geographically based.

Two areas in which the emphasis has changed significantly are in first responder training and information technology (IT). To better prepare first responders, many colleges have incorporated incident management, triage, and disaster relief elements into their curricula and have devised separate in-service programs. Although community colleges have long offered IT programming and networking, such training in institutions nationwide is now placing much greater emphasis on cybersecurity issues. Working with federal agencies such as the National Security Agency and the National Science Foundation, colleges are developing pre-service and in-service programs for professionals who will help protect the nation's information systems. Recognizing the tremendous expense of such upgrading efforts, several community colleges are developing regional training facilities that will not only prepare professionals in their own localities but will also train trainers from other institutions, who can then bring that expertise to their home institutions.

EDUCATING AND TRAINING FIRST RESPONDERS

The pre-service and in-service work at many community colleges has changed. More nursing programs, for example, deal with mass emergency issues, including triage training. Training for firefighters and police includes more elements dealing with hazardous materials and crowd control. Other institutions are extending their training beyond professional first responders to reach out to the community through programs such as service learning relating to homeland security, community discussions of homeland security issues, and volunteer programs and service centers that can respond to disasters should the need arise. These engaged and informed citizens become a second wave of assistance and defense in times of crisis.

SHARING RESOURCES AND FACILITIES

As institutions that are committed to education and training, community colleges have resources that they can share with their communities in times of crisis. Training facilities alone—from mock cities used to train police and firefighters to laboratories used to train nurses and other allied health professionals—serve a daily function within the colleges, as they educate pre-service or in-service students. In the event of a real-life crisis, they can be transformed quickly into nursing units, blood-testing laboratories, communications centers (83% of community colleges have videoconferencing facilities), and even—given existing child care, recreational, and food-producing facilities—evacuation centers or emergency shelters for the displaced. Community colleges have responded in these ways, most recently during hurricanes in 2004 and 2005. To provide training in specialized areas such as water rescue or collapsed building rescue, community colleges are investing heavily in facilities, regional and national in scope, devoted to disaster relief training.

CONCLUSION

Although homeland security has gained prominence as a national focus and investment, it is clear that much of the most effective preparation must begin at local, state, and regional levels. What this report documents is the central role community colleges are equipped to play and are quickly moving to assume in that preparation. Their responsiveness to community needs, their history of training in homeland security fields, their involvement in community planning and resource sharing, and their track record for high-quality training of first and second responders truly place them on the front line of homeland security.

COMMUNITY COLLEGES SERVING COMMUNITY NEEDS

Unlike most other institutions of higher education, community colleges are directly and explicitly linked to their communities. Their student bodies come, by and large, from local sponsoring areas. At least part of their funding comes from local sources, through sponsorship, tuition, or a combination of the two. Most community colleges—even those with a strong orientation to programs for transfer to universities—have as a part of their missions the economic and workforce development of their communities. Most have a wide range of community service programs, from adult literacy to skills upgrading to community theatre. Community colleges are vital, contributing parts of the communities that surround them. It is both logical and appropriate, as communities rethink the measures they undertake to make themselves secure, that community colleges play a central leadership role.

Because of the communications problems that occurred during the September 11 attack and Hurricane Katrina, a greater sense of urgency about coordinating responses to disasters now exists. Training for all levels of homeland security specialists, from first responders to border security patrollers, as well as preparation for possible future terrorist attacks and disasters, concern communities throughout the United States. Community colleges can, in most areas, provide cost-effective training and education that complement what the 9/11 Commission called "unified command procedures" (National Commission on Terrorist Attacks, 2004, p. 397) in ways that are appropriate to the needs and resources of their communities.

The new emphasis on homeland security and emergency preparedness has created a plethora of complex new needs in the preparation, training, and retraining of personnel, as well as in the planning, design, implementation, and coordination of security and disaster relief functions. These needs range from focused activities, like training for fire and police professionals about weapons of mass destruction (WMD), to broader, community-wide activities such as the development and coordination of emergency management plans. Whereas initial plans and funding to meet these needs are generated at the federal and state levels, most of the actual implementation, training, and operation occur at the local level. It is at the local level that the nation's community colleges are already demonstrating that they can provide essential services to help support community and national homeland security efforts.

According to the Associated Press (2004), community colleges have taken the lead in homeland security education: According to the National Center for Education Statistics (2003), 80% of police, 86% of fire fighters, and 84% of EMTs received their credentials at community colleges. Community colleges have been steadily expanding their range of homeland security services and content areas. Because these colleges already provide education and training to many professionals and have a long history of working closely with local governments and agencies to plan and implement local security training, their value to the nation's homeland security efforts is obvious, and they are likely to play an increasingly important role.

EMERGENCY PREPAREDNESS AND HOMELAND SECURITY PLANNING

The engagement of most community colleges in the work of their communities means that they are involved in more than merely providing an educated and trained workforce. Many involve themselves actively in all aspects of community development, partnering with economic development authorities as well as service organizations and social service agencies. They are involved as well in all stages of community planning, from needs assessment through training program development and delivery. Through their involvement in planning they are becoming essential elements of their communities' homeland security and disaster relief efforts.

Planning for homeland security occurs at federal, state, and local levels, and community college planning follows essentially the same pattern. At the national level, community college organizations, in particular AACC and the League for Innovation in the Community College, have developed special initiatives and are exploring ways of defining the broad functions community colleges across the nation can provide. State agencies are coordinating with these college systems within their borders to provide coherent, consistent approaches to planning and training. At the local level, individual colleges are working with government agencies within their sponsoring counties or regions to determine the best ways to meet local homeland security needs. Thus connected at multiple levels of planning, community colleges are planning and preparing to provide the most appropriate services and expertise at each level of government.

The Federal Emergency Management Agency (FEMA) has established a Web-based Emergency Management Institute at www.training.fema.gov/emiweb, which provides emergency management training courses. Another FEMA Web site, www.training.fema.gov/emiweb/edu, provides a list of colleges offering emergency management degrees, free courses for use by colleges, and other valuable information.

A number of states have extensive plans that involve community colleges at multiple levels. Iowa's plan, for example, covers a wide range of topics, from agroterrorism to security training and awareness (Dardis, 2004, 2005; see also Iowa Homeland Security, 2006). Iowa has established a network of training providers, including community colleges and the University of Iowa, to identify and meet needs for training—long-term and short-term, classroom-based and Web-based—in homeland security. State-level planning creates more localized training emphases than the more broadly based national planning can; agroterrorism, for example, is a much more significant issue in Iowa than it might be in Rhode Island.

Other states have developed coordinated state systems that use community colleges as critical components for planning and implementing homeland security strategies. Walters State Community College in Tennessee, for example, is a member of the state response team and houses a regional homeland security office. Pennsylvania's community colleges are part of regional response teams, as are Florida's, which are geared to respond to both security and natural disasters. Macomb Community College in Michigan creates and coordinates mock scenarios requiring multijurisdictional responses in the Detroit area. These regional and statewide activities make it obvious that homeland security efforts range beyond county boundaries.

Targeted planning within statewide initiatives allows for customization of programs to meet regional and local needs. Community colleges in Iowa or Kentucky can tailor state-designed and, in some cases, state-provided training to meet the particular needs of their communities, based on local characteristics, whether urban or rural, densely or sparsely populated, with agricultural, industrial, or service-based economies. The Community College of Philadelphia provides a very specialized type of regional programming, an IT security specialist training program, designed specifically for professionals who manage the security of computer networks.

Local planning and training can be part of a national planning strategy as well. Kirkwood Community College in Cedar

---

Exhibit 1

How to Plan at the Local Level
- Consult state homeland security Web sites for information about statewide planning.
- Provide information to state agencies and FEMA.
- Coordinate planning with state and local agencies.
- Assess both local and regional needs and develop programs accordingly.

Examples
- **Kirkwood Community College** (IA) provides statewide and national training.
- The **Collegiate Consortium for Workforce and Economic Development** (PA) offers specialized training in 57 different areas.
- **Howard Community College** (MD) has developed a community preparedness CD-ROM for its general population.

Rapids is part of the Iowa planning and training system, for example, but it also offers training in dealing with hazardous materials to trainers throughout the country. The Collegiate Consortium for Workforce and Economic Development (www.cctrain.org), based in Philadelphia, offers 57 homeland security training modules to any community college in the nation willing to affiliate with the consortium; affiliation provides course curricula and pedagogical assistance to community college trainers throughout the country.

Exhibit 1 (see page 2) illustrates what the League for Innovation (2006) calls "leveraging community colleges for homeland security." The examples show a growing trend toward partnerships and collaborations that plan and provide training quickly and efficiently, without forcing individual communities to develop homeland security strategies on their own.

ESTABLISHING PARTNERSHIPS

Homeland security is an expensive proposition, and planning and training for it, particularly within a relatively short time frame, is well beyond the resources of most community colleges. Thus it makes sense for colleges and agencies to collaborate and form partnerships to plan and offer training. Since 2001, numerous collaborations have developed, some of them state-sponsored, some springing from local initiatives, but all focused on providing appropriate training as effectively and efficiently as possible.

Cooperation in homeland security training offers community colleges and their localities broader and more efficient opportunities for training. At the national level, the FEMA Web-based project provides extensive information and successful strategies that invite emulation. The League for Innovation's Homeland Security Education at the Community College program offers the combined expertise of several leading community colleges in five areas: community and citizen preparedness, terrorism and homeland defense, WMD, community college leadership training, and disaster response and recovery.

Many states have developed statewide strategies that emulate national cooperation. Among them are Arkansas, Florida, Kentucky, Louisiana, Maryland, Pennsylvania, Texas, and Washington. These statewide cooperatives make a wide range of partnerships with national entities possible. St. Petersburg College (FL), for example, has partnerships with the U.S. Departments of Defense and Homeland Security, the Florida National Guard, the Office of Domestic Preparedness, and many other government agencies. Often colleges will take the lead in these efforts. Central Piedmont Community College, for example, heads North Carolina's emergency response training council.

Statewide and regional partnerships clearly offer a greater efficiency and range of services, as well as opportunities for leadership, to community colleges. As the Philadelphia Collegiate Consortium's training program illustrates, partnerships need not be initiated or sustained by national organizations or state governments alone. Many other localities are seeing individual agencies form larger, stronger, and more extensive partnerships through their local community colleges. Tarrant County College in Ft. Worth, Texas, conducts Occupational Safety and Health Administration (OSHA) conferences. Owens Community College in Ohio, through its work as a part of the Great Lakes Educational Consortium for Homeland Security and other consortia, works with more than 70 agencies to provide homeland security services and training. Meridian College in Mississippi is part of the FEMA network and an active member of the Mississippi State Anti-Terrorism Network. Riverside Community College's Ben Clark Center is working actively to provide extensive homeland security training for the former site of March Air Reserve Base.

Several colleges are working to establish permanent homeland security training and planning programs with state and federal aid. With the active support of county and local law enforcement agencies, Monroe Community College in Rochester, New York, has established a Homeland Security Management Institute designed to serve not only local and regional needs but also national needs, through a program that trains security and law enforcement trainers from around the country.

The degree of cooperation between community colleges and government agencies is extensive. Almost 50% of the respondents to AACC's survey indicated that they were actively coordinating homeland security efforts with municipal or county agencies, about 35% were working with state offices, and 12% were coordinating with the National Guard. Almost every responding college had established some kind of partnership with an external agency to provide more extensive homeland security services.

Partnerships at the local, state, and national levels offer the most significant and effective means of providing extensive homeland security training. As R. Thomas Flynn, president of Monroe Community College (NY), wrote, "Our review of homeland security and civic engagement programs in community and technical colleges nationwide reveals powerful programs in place, along with significant untapped potential. Given these findings, we should not duplicate, at great expense to the American taxpayer, education and training programs already in

place" (cited in Monroe Community College, 2003).

Because community colleges have missions that involve them with their communities at many different levels, they have not only connections within the com-

---

Exhibit 2

How to Partner to Serve Regional Needs
- Convene a summit of interested parties.
- Determine regional needs using state and regional input.
- Solicit regional partners.
- Develop a resource-sharing training plan.
- Pool resources.
- Consider using college facilities for homeland security needs.

Examples
- **Monroe Community College** (NY) established a public safety training facility in partnership with Monroe County and the City of Rochester.
- **Community College of Denver** (CO) is part of the League for Innovation's Homeland Security Education in Community Colleges project.

---

munity but also a long tradition of service. These attributes make them likely and effective candidates to call together different segments of their communities and regions to explore the possibilities of joint ventures. This convener or coordinator role has been a tradition at community colleges, but perhaps never before in the service of such important cooperation. Community colleges, which provide a relatively apolitical environment, afford a venue where the security of the community can be discussed openly and honestly.

SERVING AS EMERGENCY PREPAREDNESS AND OPERATIONS CENTERS

The partnerships outlined in the previous section illustrate the different roles that community colleges may play; one of the most important is how they use facilities for both training and emergency preparedness. When the attacks on the World Trade Center occurred, for example, the Borough of Manhattan Community College campus served as a command center for first responders. Similarly, many colleges in Florida, including Brevard, Broward, Daytona Beach, Indian River, and Polk Community Colleges and Miami Dade College, became disaster relief sites during the four successive hurricanes of 2004. These colleges are part of the Florida Community Colleges Risk Management Consortium, which coordinates responses to disasters throughout the state.

Community colleges' responses to Hurricanes Katrina and Rita in 2005 were even more extensive.

Alabama, California, and Massachusetts) either waived tuition or allowed in-state rates for out-of-state students. Other colleges, among them Bucks County (PA), Flathead Valley (MT), NorthWest Arkansas, and Santa Fe (NM) Community Colleges and Georgia Perimeter College, offered displaced students free or reduced tuition and fees.

Although the use of community college facilities during disasters might seem to be simply community-oriented responses to immediate necessities, a significant number of colleges have developed agreements and plans with their localities to fulfill special responsibilities during disasters, according to the AACC survey. Harcum College (PA), Hutchinson Community College and Area Vocational School (KS), Quinsigamond Community College (MA), and Seminole Community College (FL), are among the 34% of responding colleges designated as evacuation sites. Others have more specialized responsibilities: Arapahoe Community College (CO), Asnuntuck Community College (CT), McHenry County College (IL), and Oklahoma City Community College are all designated vaccination sites. Gaston College (NC) and Orange Coast College (CA) are nuclear decontamination sites. Many others—like Floyd College (GA), Montgomery College (TX), North Iowa Area Community College, Schenectady County Community College (NY), and Washington County Community College (ME)—are designated emergency command centers.

Although attacks like those that occurred on September 11 are likeliest to occur in large cities, the

---

Exhibit 3

How to Develop Emergency Facilities
- Work with local officials on emergency planning to determine disaster relief needs.
- Consider institutional space for possible emergency use.
- Study communications capacity for possible emergency use.
- Designate staff to serve as site coordinators.

Examples
- **Florida Community Colleges Risk Management Consortium** planned provision evacuation and shelter facilities for natural disasters and used them extensively during the 2004 hurricane season.
- **Monroe County Community College** (MI) is an emergency command center for nuclear power plant accidents.

While many colleges in and near Texas, Louisiana, and Mississippi provided disaster relief sites, others across the country offered tuition waivers and discounts to students, particularly those from the New Orleans area, who would clearly not be able to resume their educations for some time. Colleges in some states (i.e., smallest percentage of respondents (20%) reporting that they had been designated as evacuation centers during disasters were from community colleges in large metropolitan centers, whereas the largest percentage (47%) were from rural areas. This disparity is probably attributable to both the more extensive infrastructure in urban areas and the greater likelihood that community colleges perform many different community functions in rural areas. In both cases, such designations show the critical importance of community college facilities in disaster planning.

Community colleges also have communications capabilities that can be of significant value in responding to disasters. According to the AACC survey, 83% have videoconferencing capabilities and 32% have satellite uplinks; another 22% and 19%, respectively, have broadcast television and radio capability that could be used in emergencies. The majority have medical training facilities and laboratories that serve allied health programs and that can be converted to provide some medical assistance in an emergency.

TRAINING HOMELAND SECURITY AND DISASTER RELIEF PROFESSIONALS

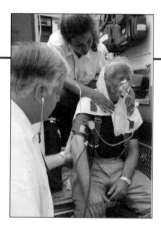

Before September 11, 2001, community colleges had already been a source of education and training for many professionals who are now central to the nation's security and disaster relief efforts. Close to 80% of first responders received all or part of their training at community colleges. More than 60% of new nurses received their training at community colleges and enhance their skills in the colleges' continuing education programs. In other areas the numbers are lower but still impressive: 36% of community colleges have programs focusing on cybersecurity; 32.4%, security and protective services; and 9.3%, counterterrorism and national security (see Figure 1).

Because community colleges had extensive experience as the primary deliverers of training for homeland security workers prior to September 11, 2001, they remain the logical choice to expand these programs to address new terrorist threats. Many institutions decided that their first response to the new homeland security needs should be to consolidate and refocus their efforts, to create new emphases and training areas, in cooperation with local and federal emergency management agencies. In Phoenix, Arizona, the Maricopa Community College Homeland Security Consortium coordinates the efforts of the system's 10 campuses and 2 skill centers with those of local agencies to develop a system of training programs that are "in direct response to the changing needs of those agencies" (Maricopa Community College Center, 2003). Maricopa was able to offer Phoenix emergency management agencies an associate of applied science (AAS)

degree and certificate programs in occupational safety and health, water resource management, and security training, as well as the following:

- law enforcement: 9 associate degree and 24 certificate programs
- fire science: 2 associate degree and 6 certificate programs
- emergency medical services: 3 AAS degree and 4 certificate programs
- hazardous materials handling: 1 AAS degree and 3 three certificate programs
- IT security: 2 AAS degree and 3 certificate programs

All of these programs can be easily updated and revised within the consortium to meet new homeland security requirements.

Similar efforts to convert past programs to address new security needs are occurring throughout the country. The Community College of Denver, for instance, has included within its public safety management AAS program an emphasis in homeland security. The Community College of Philadelphia has created an intensive 80-hour program to train IT security specialists. It has also joined with four other nearby community colleges and Drexel University to offer certification in

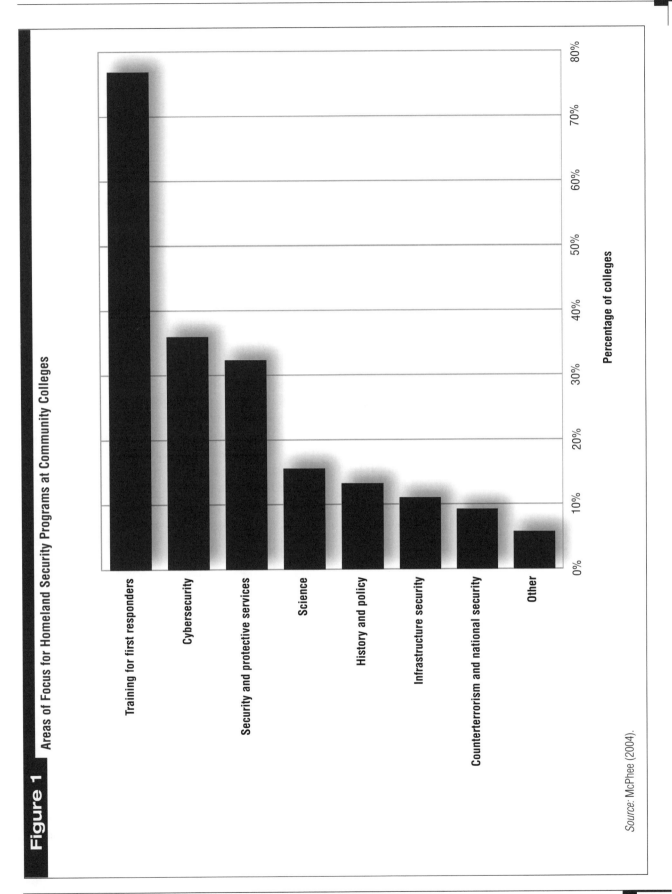

Source: McPhee (2004).

emergency management and planning to current government workers as well as to students in criminal justice and fire science. Louisiana State University at Eunice has developed a public and industrial security program.

As homeland security continues to be a focus for the nation, community colleges are likely to continue to expand programs. Almost 20% of the respondents of the AACC survey offer courses or certificates in WMD awareness and preparedness; 25% offer courses or programs in food chain management, food safety, or agroterrorism. Des Moines Area Community College's Homeland Security Emergency Management Department (IA) offers training in terrorism readiness and basic incident command, and Asheville-Buncombe Technical Community College (NC) offers an online bioterrorism incident management course. Others are initiating programs or courses in airport security training, rail and pipeline security, and mass casualty/fatality management. South Seattle Community College (WA), for example, is offering Port Authority and Transportation Security Administration (TSA) training, and Vermilion Community College (MN) is offering border patrol training. Lamar Institute of Technology (TX) has been recognized by the Coast Guard for the excellence of its maritime security training. And 6% of the colleges responding to AACC's survey (12% in large cities) offer courses, certificates, or degrees with homeland security in the title. Figure 2 details the extensive range of programs for both first and second responders, in both credit and noncredit offerings.

A number of institutions have created administrative structures designed to make access to relevant, current training available to the nation at large. Monroe Community College's Homeland Security Institute in New York is one such example. It not only trains local first responders and other security professionals but also plans to "educate other community college trainers, thereby extending its reach through the country's network of 1,100 community colleges" (Monroe Community College, 2003). Kirkwood Community

---

Exhibit 4

How to Program at the Local Level

- Review current offerings in homeland security areas.
- Develop essential regional homeland security programs for the college or in a consortium.
- Consider consolidating or revising current offerings.
- Develop unique training capabilities.
- Upgrade all continuing education training, especially in security technology.

Examples

- **Maricopa Community Colleges** (AZ) consolidated, revised, and updated all relevant programs.
- **Southwestern Community College** (IA) developed its state's first program in cybercrime.
- **Kentucky Community and Technical College System** formed a network of homeland security training throughout the state.

College (IA) has a similar OSHA train-the-trainer program. St. Petersburg Community College (FL) has developed a federally funded National Terrorism Preparedness Institute that will ultimately have broad national impact.

In some cases, the administrative structure is statewide—Kentucky and Iowa are two states with such structures—but it is important to note that the primary building blocks of the structure are the states' community colleges. Hazard Community and Technical College President Jay Box (Kentucky Community and Technical College System [KCTCS], 2004) sees the "strong presence . . . throughout the state" of Kentucky's community and technical college as a primary reason for its being the logical site for homeland security training within the state.

It is important to acknowledge these efforts and others like them at community colleges throughout the country; however, many efforts are extensions or modifications of efforts and programs that were in place for some time, although their emphases may have changed. Because community colleges have a tradition of attending to the security and health needs of their communities, their current attention to homeland security is only a logical extension of their traditional functions. State and federal agencies seem to have recognized this logic by locating and funding homeland security training initiatives at community colleges throughout the nation.

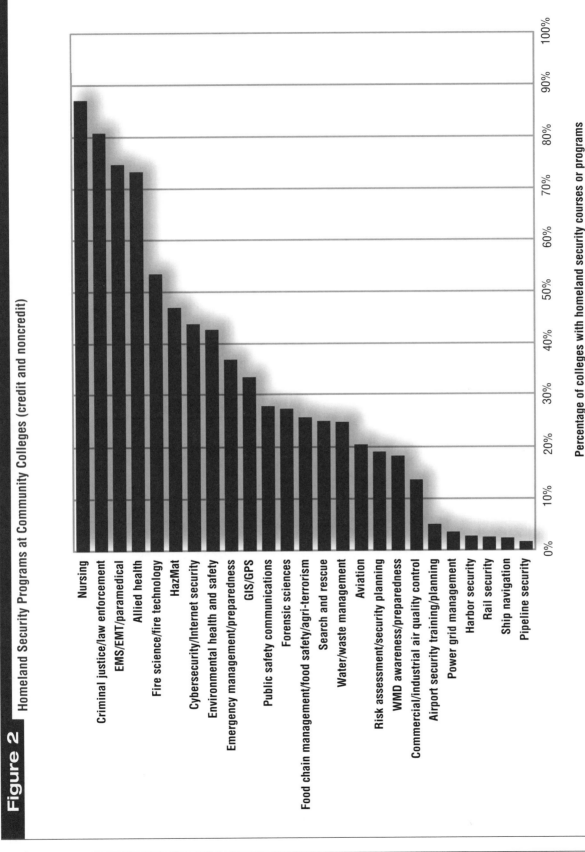

Figure 2 Homeland Security Programs at Community Colleges (credit and noncredit)

Percentage of colleges with homeland security courses or programs

Source: SRI International (2004).

Training First and Second Responders

Besides providing entry-level training for a large number of first responders in the United States, community colleges offer extensive continuing education programs for first and second responders. Some first responder education programs are being modified to include greater emphasis on terrorist activity and natural disasters. As Ronnie Day, director of Kentucky's State Fire Commission, has noted,

> We are beginning to see an increase in requests for awareness courses in terrorism and WMD as well as Community Emergency Response Team (CERT) training. In the past year, we have delivered Hazardous Materials and CERT classes to approximately 700 fire, rescue and emergency medical service personnel throughout the Commonwealth. (KCTCS, 2004)

Houston Community College System's homeland security–oriented courses for first responders include Terrorism and Facility Protection Awareness, Homeland Security Intelligence Operations for Law Enforcement Personnel, and Explosives Foundation Training for Medical Personnel.

Several community colleges, recognizing that first-response personnel in the field need to upgrade their skills in homeland security, have concentrated on providing this type of in-service training first. Thus Iowa Central Community College's Homeland Security Training Center recruits professional trainers from throughout the nation to provide hands-on training in law enforcement, firefighting, emergency medical services, public health, and emergency management. Among the courses offered in Iowa are Basic Incident Command and Emergency Response to Terrorism.

Community colleges also have come to understand that "one-shot training that is not linked in any way to a career pathway does little to provide incentives for excellence in frontline positions such as airport security screening" (Flynn, Milliron, de los Santos, & Miles, 2003). Colleges like the Community College of Denver have revised many of their first responder programs to include homeland security issues and career pathways. The college's public safety management AAS degree now includes a homeland security emphasis. In Pennsylvania's Lehigh Valley, courses in conventional criminal justice training have integrated terrorism emphases; Northampton Community College's Thomas Marakovits, head of that college's criminal justice program, said of a course called Contemporary Issues of Criminal Justice, "There was a terrorism com-

---

Exhibit 5

How to Train First Responders in Homeland Security
- Incorporate homeland security elements in current first responder degree and certificate curricula.
- Incorporate hazardous materials training where relevant.
- Expand advisory committees to include homeland security professionals.

Examples
- **Glendale Community College** (AZ) is developing a comprehensive, coordinated program of fire science, health, criminal justice, emergency management services, and environmental training.
- **Community College of Aurora** (CO) is creating a Homeland Security Training Center that will focus on WMD, tactical training, and emergency management.
- **Cuyahoga Community College District** (OH) organized its offerings by targeted stakeholders, including transportation, infrastructure, and first responders.

ponent before September 11, 2001, but it has grown to a much greater component since then" (cited in Falsone, 2004). The course now includes modules on religious fanaticism and the history of terrorism.

Tidewater Community College (VA), recognizing a different need in its relatively rural service area, has devised a way to expand its EMT services. In cooperation with Bayside High School Health Sciences Academy, it offers high school students training that will earn them basic EMT certification as well as seven college credits. Expanding the number of certified EMTs expands the range of services possible from this critical group of first responders.

In short, community colleges are responding to the homeland security training needs of first responders at the continuing education level for those already in the field while also integrating homeland security issues in their pre-service first responder programs.

COMMUNITY ENGAGEMENT PROGRAMS

Although training first responders and upgrading their skills are crucial, community colleges are doing significantly more. By establishing community engagement and awareness programs in many different areas, as well as homeland security institutes and centers, community colleges are making it clear that homeland security affects a broader group than just first responders and that the colleges are regional resources for a wide range of services and needs.

Community engagement programs can take many different forms, such as service learning programs that involve student work and internships in community service agencies, like Raritan Valley Community College's (NJ) service learning program that engages more than 200 students a semester in homeland security activities. Gulf Coast Community College (FL) stimulates citizenship skills in its students by bringing students and community members together to discuss and debate homeland security issues. Miami Dade College in Florida provides service learning opportunities within its homeland security and related programs, to make students aware of their civic responsibilities as protectors of homeland security.

Other community colleges stimulate community volunteer efforts. Wayne Community College (NC) has a volunteer agency for disaster management. The University of Hawaii— Windward Community College houses a volunteer resource center on campus for the Red Cross, Civil Defense, and other agencies. Actions such as these become catalysts for community engagement for people beyond the student population.

These efforts at developing community engagement at the program, institutional, and regional levels show how pervasive the concept of homeland security has become within community college curricula and operations. Homeland security is clearly neither an isolated element of the curriculum nor merely a part of the noncredit operation. It has become a part of daily life for many colleges.

Exhibit 6

How to Encourage Community Engagement
- Encourage faculty to include homeland security service learning programs in courses.
- Include cultural awareness and community engagement elements in homeland security courses.
- Establish volunteer community service centers.

Examples
- **Raritan Valley Community College** (NJ) incorporated service with the Red Cross in some of its courses.
- **Lakeland Community College's** (OH) campus K-9 unit is a member of the county's first response team.
- **Mineral Area College** (MO) is offering DVD-based homeland security courses to increase awareness in Missouri.

SPECIALIZED EQUIPMENT AND TRAINING FACILITIES

In some cases, community engagement is taking a more tangible form. Many community colleges have extensive specialized facilities for training related to homeland security (see Figure 3). Roughly 70% of the community colleges in the nation either own or share medical laboratories and related facilities for training, and 35% have, or have access to, firing ranges or other weapons training facilities. Twenty-three percent own or have access to burn buildings, and a surprising 10% have water rescue and 6% have industrial disaster training facilities. Several colleges (6%) even have or share mock disaster villages.

In addition to these facilities, several community colleges and localities are investing heavily in constructing new disaster training and simulation facilities. Wayne County Community College District has just opened a new facility to house the Michigan Institute for Public Safety Education, which will train first response and emergency workers, as well as provide public awareness programming. Owens Community College in Toledo, Ohio, is building a $10 million homeland security center that will include an antiterrorism simulation center as well as training areas

for a wide range of disasters, from train wrecks to collapsed buildings. In western Pennsylvania, Westmoreland County Community College is creating a 168-acre Public Safety Training Site. Kankakee Community College in Illinois is completing a regional Emergency Management Training Center; Tarrant County College District (TX) and Oakland Community College (MI) have built mock cities to train for various disaster scenarios.

Exhibit 7

How to Develop Training Facilities

- Inventory current facilities for their usefulness for homeland security training.
- Determine any additional facilities needs.
- Determine the need for specialized or regional facilities.
- Determine the fiscal practicalities of ongoing support for special facilities.

Examples

- **Owens Community College** (OH) is building a homeland security center that will include anti-terrorism simulations.
- **Oakland Community College** (MI) has a Combined Regional Emergency Services Training (CREST) facility that provides a 22-acre replica town for training and simulation exercises.
- **Tarrant County College District** (TX) constructed a Public Safety Institute.
- **Western Piedmont Community College** (NC) is building an emergency services training center.

PROTECTING INFORMATION, NETWORKS, AND INFRASTRUCTURE

As our society and infrastructure have become increasingly dependent on technology, the need to focus greater attention on the security of information and IT has become more acute. AACC was among the first higher education organizations to seize on this issue. In partnership with the National Science Foundation, it convened a conference of

national cybersecurity experts in June 2002 to define and support the role of community colleges in cybersecurity education. As AACC President George Boggs (AACC, 2002) noted in remarks to that group, we need IT workers who are skilled in computer network defense, business continuity, disaster recovery, critical infrastructure protection, and information assurance:

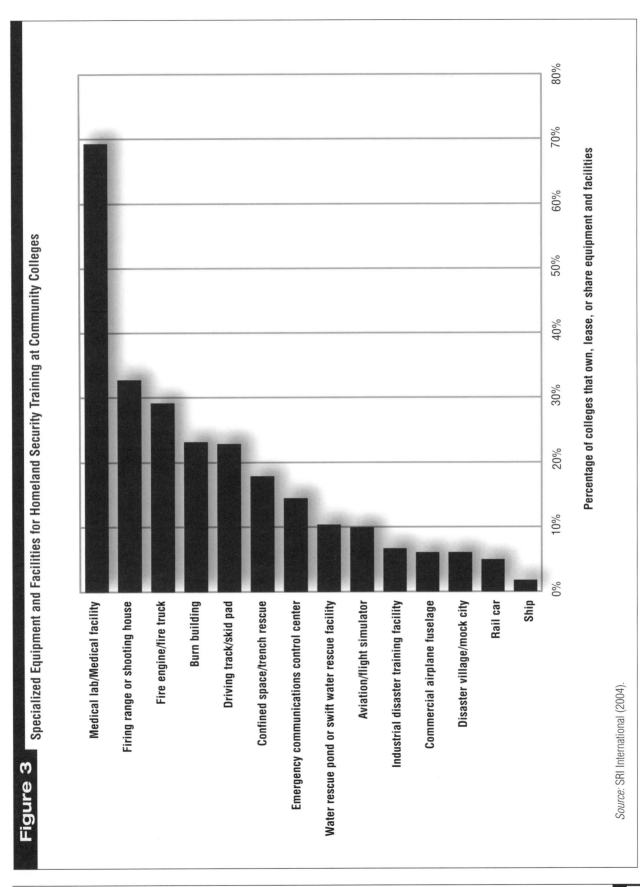

Figure 3 Specialized Equipment and Facilities for Homeland Security Training at Community Colleges

Percentage of colleges that own, lease, or share equipment and facilities

Source: SRI International (2004).

Even in today's difficult economy, the demand for cybersecurity professionals is outstripping supply. High-tech companies and government agencies are using innovative programs to recruit and train workers with specialized skills in information security. America needs educational programs to prepare the IT workers of the future to maintain the security of our systems, and that is where community colleges come into the picture. (p. 11)

An extensive list of recommendations, documented in *Protecting Information: The Role of Community Colleges in Cybersecurity Education* (AACC, 2002), is predicated on collaborations between community colleges and other stakeholders, including 4-year colleges and universities, business and industry leaders, professional societies and trade associations, and government agencies. Those recommendations included the following:

- Form partnerships with all other stakeholders to pool resources and tap the resources of vendors, IT user communities, and government agencies.
- Coordinate educational programs.
- Identify the next generation of cybersecurity jobs and develop programs to train for them.
- Educate the college community, both internal and external, in cybersecurity issues.
- Provide continuing education for cybersecurity professionals.
- Integrate cybersecurity concepts and topics into all relevant curricula.
- Develop "reverse transfer" programs to provide applied skills to holders of bachelor's degrees.
- Use professionals in the cybersecurity field as professors and program advisors, as well as monitors of cybersecurity implementation on campus.
- Work with professional organizations to update faculty and enrich student learning.
- Seek state and federal funding for this vital but very expensive initiative. (pp. 31–37)

Many community colleges have responded to the task force's suggestions with alacrity. Many—such as Marshall Community and Technical College (WV), Inver Hills Community College (MN), and the University of Hawaii—Honolulu Community College—offer network security certification programs. Others, such as Miami Dade College (FL) and Oklahoma City Community College, are offering programs in cybersecurity; Tulsa Community College (OK) trains its faculty in cybersecurity at the University of Tulsa, then offers cybersecurity courses on its campus. Clover Park Technical College (WA) is one of the National Security Agency–certified institutions in the west to offer cybersecurity training. In addition, the National Science Foundation has designated Moraine Valley Community College (IL) as a center for systems security and information assurance, as well as Springfield Technical Community College (MA) as a center for information and telecommunications technology.

As the use of electronic data storage and transmission expands and the use of the Internet becomes even more pervasive, cybersecurity education and training will most likely become an increasingly important part of homeland security. Community colleges, with their ability to connect with many different constituencies within the communities, as well as their ability to develop excellent training programs quickly and efficiently, are an ideal venue for meeting those challenges.

Exhibit 8

How to Develop Cybersecurity Programs
- Develop an internal, institutional cybersecurity plan.
- Determine external cybersecurity training needs.
- Partner with other colleges and businesses.
- Develop certification programs for faculty and others with computer or IT degrees.

Examples
- **Springfield Technical Community College** (MA) established the National Center for Telecommunications Technicians for advanced training in information and communications technology.
- **Moraine Valley Community College** (IL) established an advanced technology center focused on systems security and information assurance.

CONCLUSION

The events of September 11, 2001, changed the nation in many profound ways, not the least of which was focusing its attention on homeland security. Failures in preparing for and dealing with the natural disasters of 2005 are likely to increase the nation's focus on disaster planning and relief as well. As localities, states, and the federal government ponder strategies for dealing with both human-made and natural disasters, the need for well-trained, current, professional first and second responders is likely to become even more obvious. That need for current, ongoing training and education can be assisted by the nation's community colleges.

This report illustrates that community colleges are already providing training and education in homeland security areas for their communities and, in several cases, for much wider populations of professionals. They are also engaged throughout the country in emergency planning and relief. Because they are community based, they also can offer resources and facilities in times of community need.

By tradition and design, community colleges adapt to and provide for emergent needs. It is clear that disaster preparedness has become a critical need, and community colleges around the country are proving that they can address that need. That better planning, coordination, and relief for disasters is necessary is beyond dispute. That community colleges can help provide resources for planning, coordination, and training of disaster prevention and relief professionals should be evident as well. Community colleges have an important role to play in the development of effective systems to handle disasters. They are indeed on the front lines of the nation's efforts to cope with human-made and natural disasters.

References

American Association of Community Colleges. (2002). *Protecting information: The role of community colleges in cybersecurity education.* Washington, DC: Community College Press.

Associated Press. (2004, February 6). *The leader in homeland security education.* Available from www.cnn.com/2004/EDUCATION/02/06/ community.colleges.ap

Dardis, R. (2004). *The Iowa homeland security strategy.* Des Moines, IA: Iowa Homeland Security and Emergency Management. Available from www.iowahomelandsecurity.org

Dardis, R. (2005). *The Iowa homeland security strategy.* Des Moines, IA: Iowa Homeland Security and Emergency Management. Available from www.iowahomelandsecurity.org

Falsone, N. (2004, February 29). NCC doing its bit for homeland security. *The Express-Times,* p. B-1.

Flynn, R. T., Milliron, M. D., de los Santos, G. E., & Miles, C. L. (2003, July). Homeland security and the community college: A vibrant present and a vital future. *Leadership Abstracts, 16*(7). Available from www.league.org

Iowa Homeland Security and Emergency Management. (2006). *Iowa: Secure & prepared.* Available from www.iowahomelandsecurity.org/asp/HS_inIowa/ HSEM_info.asp

Kentucky Community and Technical College System. (2004, March 1). *KCTCS develops homeland security program* [News release]. Available from www.kctcs.net/newspublications

League for Innovation in the Community College. (2006). *Leveraging community colleges for homeland security.* Available from www.league.org/league/projects/homeland_ security/vision_purpose.html

Maricopa Community Colleges Center for Workforce Development. (2003, February). *Homeland security programs* [Executive summary]. Available from www.maricopa.edu

McPhee, S. (2004). *Hot programs at community colleges* [Research brief]. Washington, DC: American Association of Community Colleges.

Monroe Community College. (2003, December 9). *MCC launches Homeland Security Institute.* Available from www.monroecc.edu

National Center for Educational Statistics. (2003). *Integrated postsecondary education data system (IPEDS) completion survey* [Data file]. Washington, DC: U.S. Department of Education.

National Commission on Terrorist Attacks. (2004). *The 9/11 Commission report: Final report of the National Commission on Terrorist Attacks Upon the United States* (authorized edition). New York: Norton.

SRI International. (2004). *AACC survey on homeland security and related issues* [Aggregated responses]. Washington, DC: American Association of Community Colleges. Available from www.aacc.nche.edu/homelandsecurityreports

Additional Resources

WEB SITES

Collegiate Consortium for Workforce and Economic
   Development Programs
www.cctrain.org

Community College of Philadelphia (homeland security)
www.ccp.edu/home/workforce/homeland_security.html

Department of Homeland Security, Federal Emergency
   Management Agency, U.S. Fire Administration,
   Emergency Management Institute
www.training.fema.gov/emiweb
www.training.fema.gov/emiweb/edu

Florida Community Colleges Risk Management
   Consortium
www.fccrmc.com

Monroe Community College
Homeland Security Management Institute
www.monroecc.edu/depts/hsmi

Pierce College
Center of Excellence for Homeland Security
www.pierce.ctc.edu/HomelandSecurity/education/
   listCTC.php

Springfield Technical Community College
National Center for Telecommunications Technologies
www.nctt.org

Tarrant County College-Northwest
Public Safety Institute
www.tccd.edu/neutral/DivisionDepartmentPage.asp?
   pagekey=31&menu=2

PUBLICATIONS

Barth, R. (2004, September 28). Iowa college to train
   responders for agroterrorism: $3.2 million grant
   from Department of Homeland Security funds
   program to protect food supply. *Community
   College Times.*

Blezard, R. (2003, February/March). Safe and secure:
   Community colleges in the post–9/11 world.
   Community College Journal, pp. 10–13.

Cohen, B. (2003, December 15). *Local colleges unite
   for homeland security.* Available from
   www.thereporteronline.com

Gamble, C. (2004, September 28). Community colleges develop programs and strategy. *Community
   College Times.*

Holmes, N. (2004, January 20). Cybersecurity funding looks favorable. *Community College Times.*

Holmes, N. (2004, February 3). AACC meets with
   homeland security official. *Community
   College Times.*

Holmes, N. (2004, March 16). Phenomenal growth seen
   in homeland security. *Community College Times.*

Holmes, N. (2004, October 26). 2-year colleges take lead
   in homeland security. *Community College Times.*

Johnson, E. A. (2003, February/March). Biosecurity—
   The Bio-Link Project. *Community College Journal,*
   pp. 18–20.

Kabat Lensch, E. (2003, February/March). The fight against terrorism. *Community College Journal,* pp. 14–17.

LaRose, M. (2004, May 11). National security at stake in changing world. *Community College Times.*

LaRose, M. (2004, September 28). AACC launches flight crew defense training course to be expanded nationwide at 2-year colleges. *Community College Times.*

Neyman, J. (2004, August 24). Colleges embrace homeland security curriculum. *USA Today.* Available from www.usatoday.com/news/education/2004-08-24-homeland-usat_x.htm

Perez, A. (2004, September 28). Lesson learned from 9/11: Be prepared. *Community College Times.*

Shek, K. (2004, August 3). Kentucky colleges to add more homeland security training. *Community College Times.*

Smith, L., & Miller, D. (2002). *Before crisis hits.* Washington, DC: Community College Press.

Teles, E. J., & Hovis, R. C. (2003, February/March). Community colleges and cybersecurity education. *Community College Journal,* pp. 22–25.

Appendix A:
AACC Survey on Homeland Security and Related Issues (2004)

Survey Cover Letter

Dear [title and name]:

The American Association of Community Colleges (AACC) needs your assistance. AACC is working to showcase to Congress and federal agencies the importance of community colleges in homeland security efforts. You can help in this effort by completing our survey on homeland security and related issues for your institution (or by forwarding this message to a colleague who can complete it). The questionnaire can be accessed by clicking on the link below or by copying and pasting this URL into your browser.

[insert hyperlink to questionnaire]

The greater the number of community colleges that respond to this survey, the more powerful and cogent the story we can tell about how community colleges serve as key homeland security assets in local communities, regions, and the nation.

Community colleges are known to provide programs and services in security and public safety, as well as nursing and allied health. In order to provide a more complete picture of homeland security programs and facilities, we ask that you think beyond the traditional first responder programs offered by your college. Homeland security also covers a broad spectrum of related programs: cyber security, emergency management, pipeline management, power grid management, food safety, transportation security, and water/waste water management, to name a few. AACC recognizes some colleges have contracts with military, intelligence, or other entities that are sensitive in nature. If you have such contracts, please complete the questionnaire as far as possible, leaving out only the item(s) you consider confidential.

AACC, working with SRI International, developed this survey on homeland security and related issues. The analysis and report will provide a picture of what assets community colleges have in homeland security programs. The report will present aggregate data, as well as descriptions of unique facilities and programs, and will be made available to all survey respondents.

In addition to the questionnaire, we're also collecting handouts and brochures that focus on homeland security programs or specialized training equipment. If you have any such materials, please send them to Laurie Quarles. Please do not send a general course catalogue. Laurie's mailing address is: Laurie Quarles, AACC, One Dupont Circle, NW, Suite 410, Washington, DC 20036. Her phone number is (202) 728-0200, ext. 249.

If you have questions or need further information about the survey, please contact the SRI project leader.

Thank you for your prompt attention.

Sincerely,
George Boggs
President and CEO
American Association of Community Colleges

If your college—as identified above—includes multiple campuses, please include information on all campuses in your responses.

PROGRAMS AND COURSES

1. In which of the following areas, if any, does your college offer or plan to offer a degree program, a certificate program, or course(s)? Please include **both** credit and non-credit offerings.

(PLEASE SELECT ALL THAT APPLY IN EACH ROW)

		Offer degree programs in this area	Offer certificate programs in this area	Offer courses in thisarea, but no certificate or degree	Currently planning to initiate/ expand offerings in this area	No current offerings & no plans for offerings in this area
a.	Airport security training/planning	1	2	3	4	5
b.	Allied health (includes dental hygienists, medical technologists, physical therapy assistants, radiology technicians, etc.) Does NOT include nursing.	1	2	3	4	5
c.	Aviation (mechanics/pilots/ avionics)	1	2	3	4	5
d.	Commercial/industrial air quality control	1	2	3	4	5
e.	Criminal justice/law enforcement	1	2	3	4	5
f.	Cyber security/internet security	1	2	3	4	5
g.	Emergency management/preparedness	1	2	3	4	5
h.	Emergency medical service/emergency medical technician/paramedic	1	2	3	4	5
i.	Environmental health and safety	1	2	3	4	5
j.	Fire science/fire technology	1	2	3	4	5
k.	Food chain management, food safety, or agri-terrorism	1	2	3	4	5
l.	Forensic sciences	1	2	3	4	5
m.	GIS/GPS	1	2	3	4	5
n.	Harbor security	1	2	3	4	5
o.	HazMat	1	2	3	4	5
p.	Nursing	1	2	3	4	5
q.	Pipeline security	1	2	3	4	5
r.	Power grid management	1	2	3	4	5

1. **(continued)** In which of the following areas, if any, does your college offer or plan to offer a degree program, a certificate program, or course(s)? Please include **both** credit and non-credit offerings.
(**PLEASE SELECT ALL THAT APPLY IN EACH ROW**)

		Offer degree programs in this area	Offer certificate programs in this area	Offer courses in thisarea, but no certificate or degree	Currently planning to initiate/ expand offerings in this area	No current offerings & no plans for offerings in this area
s.	Public safety communications	1	2	3	4	5
t.	Rail security	1	2	3	4	5
u.	Risk assessment/security planning	1	2	3	4	5
v.	Search and rescue	1	2	3	4	5
w.	Ship navigation	1	2	3	4	5
x.	Water/waste water management	1	2	3	4	5
y.	WMD awareness/preparedness	1	2	3	4	5

2. Does your college offer a course, certificate, or degree in which "homeland security" is part of the title?
(**PLEASE SELECT ALL THAT APPLY**)

Yes, course(s), but not a certificate or degree ... 1 ➔ *Please describe below*
Yes, certificate(s) .... 2 ➔ *Please describe below*
Yes, degree(s) .... 3 ➔ *Please describe below*
No, none of the above 4

If yes, what are the title(s) and general topics covered in your "homeland security" course(s)/program?

_____

_____

3. (**Besides those indicated in questions 1 and 2,** does your college offer any **other** courses, certificates, or degrees that you believe have significant homeland security components?
(**PLEASE SELECT ALL THAT APPLY**)

Yes, course(s), but not a certificate or degree ... 1 ➔ *Please describe below*
Yes, certificate(s) .... 2 ➔ *Please describe below*
Yes, degree(s) .... 3 ➔ *Please describe below*
No, none of the above 4

_____

_____

FACILITIES/EQUIPMENT

4. Which of the following training facilities or specialized equipment does your college own/lease, share with other entities, or expect to acquire within the next 12 months? (Please include facilities/equipment <u>not</u> now used for homeland security-related purposes as well as those that are used for such purposes.)
(PLEASE SELECT ALL THAT APPLY IN EACH ROW)

		Our college is sole owner/ lessee of this	Our college shares this with other entities	Our college will have this within the next 12 months	Do not have this & do not plan to have this
a.	Aviation/flight simulators	1	2	3	4
b.	Burn building(s)	1	2	3	4
c.	Commercial airplane fuselage	1	2	3	4
d.	Confined space/trench rescue	1	2	3	4
e.	Disaster village/mock city	1	2	3	4
f.	Driving track/skid pad	1	2	3	4
g.	Emergency communications control center	1	2	3	4
h.	Fire engine/fire truck for training purposes	1	2	3	4
i.	Firing range or shoot house	1	2	3	4
j.	Industrial disaster training facility	1	2	3	4
k.	Medical labs or other medical facilities for training purposes	1	2	3	4
l.	Rail car for training exercises	1	2	3	4
m.	Training ship	1	2	3	4
n.	Water rescue pond or swift water rescue facility	1	2	3	4

5. Which of the following communication capabilities, if any, does your college have?
(PLEASE SELECT ALL THAT APPLY)

Broadcast radio 1
Broadcast television 2
Satellite uplink (transmitter) 3
Video conferencing 4
Other specialized communication capabilities
(please describe below) 5
None of the above 6

Other specialized communication capabilities: _____

_____

6. Does your college own/lease or share specialized **simulation** equipment or facilities that you believe is/are related to homeland security, other than equipment/facilities specified above? (**PLEASE SELECT ONE**)

Yes .... 1 → *Please describe below*
No 2

_____

_____

7. If your college owns/leases or shares **other training or specialized equipment or facilities** that you believe is/are related to homeland security besides those listed in the above question, please describe:

_____

_____

EXCEPTIONAL FEATURES OF YOUR PROGRAMS/FACILITIES

8. If there are any features of your college's homeland security-related programs or facilities that you believe are exceptional or of particular significance, please describe them here.

_____

_____

HOMELAND SECURITY PARTNERSHIPS OR COOPERATIVE EFFORTS

9. Is your college coordinating with any of the following on any homeland security-related efforts? (**PLEASE SELECT ALL THAT APPLY**)

Other colleges 1
National Guard 2
Other military 3
Non-military federal government offices/agencies 4
State government offices/agencies 5
Municipal or county offices/agencies 6
Industry/commercial organizations 7
Other entities 8
No, none of the above 9

Please provide a brief description of your coordination activities (if any) here:

_____

_____

10. Has your college been designated as having any kind of special responsibilities during or following a natural or manmade disaster? (PLEASE SELECT ALL THAT APPLY)

> Yes, campus is an evacuation site 1
> Yes, other special responsibilities . . . . 2 ➔ *Please describe below*
> No 3

_____

_____

11. Has your college been designated by a government entity as having any kind of special **training** responsibilities that are related to homeland security? (PLEASE SELECT ONE)

> Yes . . . . 1 ➔ *Please describe below*
> No 2

_____

_____

OTHER

12. If there is anything else that your college is doing that is related to homeland security, please describe it here.

_____

_____

13. Comments.

_____

_____

14. If we have questions about your responses, whom should we contact?

Name: _____

Title: _____

E-mail address: _____

Telephone: (_____)_____ ext. _____

If you would like to print a copy of your responses, please select "Print" on your browser's "File" menu.

Thank you very much for your participation in this survey.
A report presenting aggregate survey data as well as descriptions of unique facilities and programs will be made available to all survey respondents.

Appendix B:
Survey Participants

College	State	College	State
Abraham Baldwin Agricultural College	GA	Bossier Parish Community College	LA
Adirondack Community College	NY	Bowling Green Technical College	KY
Aiken Technical College	SC	Brevard Community College	FL
Aims Community College	CO	Briarwood College	CT
Alabama Southern Community College	AL	Bristol Community College	MA
Alamance Community College	NC	Brookhaven College	TX
Albany Technical College	GA	Broward Community College	FL
Albuquerque Technical Vocational Institute	NM	Brunswick Community College	NC
Allegany College of Maryland	MD	Bucks County Community College	PA
Allen County Community College	KS	Bunker Hill Community College	MA
Alpena Community College	MI	Burlington County College	NJ
Alvin Community College	TX	Butler County Community College	PA
Amarillo College	TX	Butler County Community College	KS
American River College	CA	Cabrillo College	CA
Ancilla College	IN	Caldwell Community College and Technical Institute	NC
Andover College	ME	Calhoun Community College	AL
Anne Arundel Community College	MD	Canada College	CA
Anoka-Ramsey Community College	MN	Cankdeska Cikana Community College	ND
Arapahoe Community College	CO	Cape Cod Community College	MA
Arizona Western College	AZ	Cape Fear Community College	NC
Arkansas Northeastern College	AR	Carl Albert State College	OK
Arkansas State University-Newport	AR	Carl Sandburg College	IL
Art Institute of Seattle	WA	Carolinas College of Health Sciences	NC
Asheville-Buncombe Technical Community College	NC	Carroll Community College	MD
Ashland Community and Technical College	KY	Carteret Community College	NC
Asnuntuck Community College	CT	Cascadia Community College	WA
Athens Technical College	GA	Casper College	WY
Atlanta Metropolitan College	GA	Catawba Valley Community College	NC
Atlantic Cape Community College	NJ	Cayuga County Community College	NY
Austin Community College	TX	Cecil Community College	MD
Bainbridge College	GA	Cedar Valley College	TX
Barton County Community College	KS	Central Arizona College	AZ
Baton Rouge Community College	LA	Central Community College	NE
Bay Mills Community College	MI	Central Florida Community College	FL
Bay State College	MA	Central Georgia Technical College	GA
Beaufort County Community College	NC	Central Lakes College	MN
Bellevue Community College	WA	Central Maine Medical Center School of Nursing	ME
Bellingham Technical College	WA	Central Oregon Community College	OR
Bergen Community College	NJ	Central Piedmont Community College	NC
Berkshire Community College	MA	Central Texas College	TX
Big Sandy Community and Technical College	KY	Central Virginia Community College	VA
Bismarck State College	ND	Central Wyoming College	WY
Black Hawk College	IL	Centralia College	WA
Blackhawk Technical College	WI	Century College	MN
Bladen Community College	NC	Cerritos College	CA
Blinn College	TX	Cerro Coso Community College	CA
Blue Ridge Community College	NC	Chaffey College	CA
Borough of Manhattan Community College	NY	Chandler-Gilbert Community College	AZ

College	State	College	State
Chattahoochee Technical College	GA	Cossatot Community College of the University of Arkansas	AR
Chattahoochee Valley Community College	AL		
Chattanooga State Technical Community College	TN	County College of Morris	NJ
Chemeketa Community College	OR	Cowley County Community College	KS
Chesapeake College	MD	Crafton Hills College	CA
Chipola College	FL	Cuesta College	CA
Chippewa Valley Technical College	WI	Cuyahoga Community College District	OH
Cincinnati State Technical and Community College	OH	Cuyamaca College	CA
		Cy-Fair College	TX
Cisco Junior College	TX	Cypress College	CA
Citrus College	CA	Dabney S Lancaster Community College	VA
City College of San Francisco	CA	Dakota County Technical College	MN
Clarendon College	TX	Danville Area Community College	IL
Clark College	WA	Danville Community College	VA
Clark State Community College	OH	Darton College	GA
Clatsop Community College	OR	Davidson County Community College	NC
Cleveland Community College	NC	Davis College	OH
Clinton Community College	IA	Dawson Community College	MT
Cloud County Community College	KS	Daytona Beach Community College	FL
Clover Park Technical College	WA	Dean College	MA
Coahoma Community College	MS	Deep Springs College	NV
Coastal Bend College	TX	DeKalb Technical College	GA
Coastal Carolina Community College	NC	Delaware Technical & Community College-Stanton/Wilmington	DE
Coastal Georgia Community College	GA		
Coastline Community College	CA	Delta College	MI
Cochise College	AZ	Des Moines Area Community College	IA
Coconino Community College	AZ	Diablo Valley College	CA
Coffeyville Community College and Area Technical School	KS	Dine' College	AZ
		Dixie State College of Utah	UT
College of DuPage	IL	Dodge City Community College	KS
College of Eastern Utah	UT	Don Bosco Technical Institute	CA
College of Lake County	IL	Dunwoody College of Technology	MN
College of Marin	CA	Durham Technical Community College	NC
College of Menominee Nation	WI	Dutchess Community College	NY
College of San Mateo	CA	Dyersburg State Community College	TN
College of Southern Idaho	ID	East Arkansas Community College	AR
College of Southern Maryland	MD	East Central College	MO
College of the Desert	CA	East Central Community College	MS
College of the Mainland	TX	East Georgia College	GA
College of the Redwoods District	CA	East Los Angeles College	CA
College of the Siskiyous	CA	Eastern Arizona College	AZ
Columbia Gorge Community College	OR	Eastern Idaho Technical College	ID
Columbia State Community College	TN	Eastern Maine Community College	ME
Columbia-Greene Community College	NY	Eastern New Mexico University-Roswell	NM
Columbus State Community College	OH	Eastern Oklahoma State College	OK
Columbus Technical College	GA	Eastern Shore Community College	VA
Community College of Aurora	CO	Eastern Wyoming College	WY
Community College of Beaver County	PA	Eastfield College	TX
Community College of Denver	CO	Edgecombe Community College	NC
Community College of Philadelphia	PA	El Centro College	TX
Community College of Rhode Island	RI	El Paso Community College District	TX
Community College of the Air Force	AL	Elgin Community College	IL
Compton Community College	CA	Elizabethtown Community and Technical College	KY
Connors State College	OK	Enterprise-Ozark Community College	AL
Coosa Valley Technical College	GA	Erie Community College	NY
Copiah-Lincoln Community College	MS	Essex County College	NJ

College	State	College	State
Estrella Mountain Community College	AZ	Hartnell College	CA
Everett Community College	WA	Hawkeye Community College	IA
Evergreen Valley College	CA	Hazard Community College	KY
Fashion Institute of Technology	NY	Heartland Community College	IL
Fayetteville Technical Community College	NC	Hennepin Technical College	MN
Feather River College	CA	Hesston College	KS
Finger Lakes Community College	NY	Highland Community College	KS
Fisher College	MA	Highland Community College	IL
Florence-Darlington Technical College	SC	Highline Community College	WA
Florida Community College at Jacksonville	FL	Hill College	TX
Forsyth Technical Community College	NC	Hillsborough Community College	FL
Fort Belknap College	MT	Hocking Technical College	OH
Fort Scott Community College	KS	Holyoke Community College	MA
Fox Valley Technical College	WI	Hopkinsville Community College	KY
Frank Phillips College	TX	Horry-Georgetown Technical College	SC
Frederick Community College	MD	Hostos Community College	NY
Front Range Community College	CO	Housatonic Community College	CT
Fullerton College	CA	Houston Community College System	TX
Fulton-Montgomery Community College	NY	Howard College	TX
Gadsden State Community College	AL	Howard Community College	MD
Gainesville College	GA	Hudson County Community College	NJ
Galveston College	TX	Hutchinson Community College and	
Garden City Community College	KS	Area Vocational School	KS
Garrett College	MD	Idaho State University	ID
Gaston College	NC	Ilisagvik College	AK
Gateway Community and Technical College	KY	Illinois Central College	IL
Gateway Community College	CT	Illinois Valley Community College	IL
Gateway Technical College	WI	Imperial Valley College	CA
Gavilan College	CA	Independence Community College	KS
Genesee Community College	NY	Indian Hills Community College	IA
Georgia Highlands College	GA	Indian River Community College	FL
Georgia Military College	GA	Inver Hills Community College	MN
Georgia Perimeter College	GA	Iowa Lakes Community College	IA
Germanna Community College	VA	Iowa Western Community College	IA
Glen Oaks Community College	MI	Irvine Valley College	CA
Glendale Community College	AZ	Isothermal Community College	NC
Gloucester County College	NJ	Itasca Community College	MN
Gogebic Community College	MI	J F Drake State Technical College	AL
Goodwin College	CT	Jackson Community College	MI
Gordon College	GA	Jackson State Community College	TN
Grays Harbor College	WA	James A. Rhodes State College	OH
Grayson County College	TX	James Sprunt Community College	NC
Great Basin College	NV	Jamestown Business College	NY
Green River Community College	WA	Jamestown Community College	NY
Greenfield Community College	MA	Jefferson College	MO
Greenville Technical College	SC	Jefferson Community and Technical College	KY
Grossmont College	CA	Jefferson Community College	NY
Guilford Technical Community College	NC	Jefferson Davis Community College	AL
Gulf Coast Community College	FL	Jefferson State Community College	AL
Gwinnett Technical College	GA	John A Logan College	IL
H Councill Trenholm State Technical College	AL	John Tyler Community College	VA
Halifax Community College	NC	John Wood Community College	IL
Harcum College	PA	Johnson County Community College	KS
Harford Community College	MD	Johnston Community College	NC
Harold Washington College	IL	Joliet Junior College	IL
Harrisburg Area Community College	PA	Jones County Junior College	MS

College	State	College	State
Kalamazoo Valley Community College	MI	MacCormac Junior College	IL
Kankakee Community College	IL	Macomb Community College	MI
Kaskaskia College	IL	Madison Area Technical College	WI
Kellogg Community College	MI	Madisonville Community College	KY
Kennedy-King College	IL	Malcolm X College	IL
Kettering College of Medical Arts	OH	Manatee Community College	FL
Kilgore College	TX	Manor Junior College	PA
Kilian Community College	SD	Maria College	NY
Kingsborough Community College	NY	Marion Technical College	OH
Kirkwood Community College	IA	Marshall Community & Technical College	WV
Kirtland Community College	MI	Martin Community College	NC
Klamath Community College	OR	Marymount College	CA
L E Fletcher Technical Community College	LA	Massachusetts Bay Community College	MA
Labette Community College	KS	Massasoit Community College	MA
Lackawanna Junior College	PA	Maysville Community & Technical College	KY
LaGuardia Community College	NY	McHenry County College	IL
Lake Area Technical Institute	SD	McLennan Community College	TX
Lake Land College	IL	Mendocino College	CA
Lake Michigan College	MI	Merced College	CA
Lake Region State College	ND	Mercy College of Health Sciences	IA
Lake Tahoe Community College	CA	Meridian Community College	MS
Lake Washington Technical College	WA	Merritt College	CA
Lakeland Community College	OH	Mesa Community College	AZ
Lakeshore Technical College	WI	Metropolitan Community College	NE
Lake-Sumter Community College	FL	Miami Dade College	FL
Lamar Community College	CO	Mid-Michigan Community College	MI
Lamar Institute of Technology	TX	Middle Georgia College	GA
Lamar State College-Orange	TX	Middle Georgia Technical College	GA
Landmark College	VT	Middlesex Community College	MA
Lansing Community College	MI	Middlesex Community College	CT
Laramie County Community College	WY	Midland College	TX
Laredo Community College	TX	Mid-State Technical College	WI
Las Positas College	CA	Miles Community College	MT
Lassen Community College	CA	Milwaukee Area Technical College	WI
Lee College	TX	Mineral Area College	MO
Lenoir Community College	NC	Minneapolis Community and Technical College	MN
Lester L Cox College of Nursing and Health Sciences	MO	Minnesota West Community and Technical College	MN
		Minot State University-Bottineau	ND
Lewis and Clark Community College	IL	Mira Costa College	CA
Lincoln Land Community College	IL	Mississippi Gulf Coast Community College	MS
Linn State Technical College	MO	Missouri State University-West Plains	MO
Linn-Benton Community College	OR	Mitchell Community College	NC
Little Big Horn College	MT	Mitchell Technical Institute	SD
Lorain County Community College	OH	Moberly Area Community College	MO
Lord Fairfax Community College	VA	Modesto Junior College	CA
Los Angeles City College	CA	Mohave Community College	AZ
Los Angeles Harbor College	CA	Mohawk Valley Community College	NY
Los Angeles Trade-Technical College	CA	Monroe Community College	NY
Los Angeles Valley College	CA	Monroe County Community College	MI
Los Medanos College	CA	Montana State University-Great Falls College of Technology	MT
Louisburg College	NC		
Louisiana State University-Eunice	LA	Montcalm Community College	MI
Lower Columbia College	WA	Monterey Peninsula College	CA
Luna Community College	NM	Montgomery College	TX
Lurleen B Wallace Community College	AL	Montgomery College-Germantown	MD
Luzerne County Community College	PA	Montgomery Community College	NC

College	State	College	State
Montgomery County Community College	PA	Northwest College	WY
Moraine Park Technical College	WI	Northwest Indian College	WA
Moraine Valley Community College	IL	Northwest Iowa Community College	IA
Morgan Community College	CO	Northwest State Community College	OH
Motlow State Community College	TN	Northwestern Business College	IL
Mott Community College	MI	Northwestern Michigan College	MI
Mountain Empire Community College	VA	Northwestern Technical College	GA
Mt Hood Community College	OR	Nunez Community College	LA
Murray State College	OK	Oakland Community College	MI
Muskegon Community College	MI	Oakton Community College	IL
Napa Valley College	CA	Ocean County College	NJ
Nash Community College	NC	Odessa College	TX
Nashville State Technical Institute	TN	Ogeechee Technical College	GA
Nassau Community College	NY	Oglala Lakota College	SD
National Park Community College	AR	Okaloosa-Walton College	FL
Navarro College	TX	Oklahoma City Community College	OK
Neosho County Community College	KS	Oklahoma State University-Oklahoma City	OK
New Hampshire Community Technical		Oklahoma State University-Okmulgee	OK
College-Manchester	NH	Olive-Harvey College	IL
New Mexico Junior College	NM	Onondaga Community College	NY
New Mexico State University-Alamogordo	NM	Orange Coast College	CA
New Mexico State University-Carlsbad	NM	Orange County Community College	NY
Niagara County Community College	NY	Oregon Coast Community College	OR
North Arkansas College	AR	Otero Junior College	CO
North Central Michigan College	MI	Ouachita Technical College	AR
North Central Missouri College	MO	Owens Community College	OH
North Central State College	OH	Owensboro Community College and	
North Country Community College	NY	Technical College	KY
North Dakota State College of Science	ND	Oxnard College	CA
North Florida Community College	FL	Ozarka College	AR
North Georgia Technical College	GA	Ozarks Technical Community College	MO
North Harris College	TX	Palm Beach Community College	FL
North Idaho College	ID	Palo Verde College	CA
North Iowa Area Community College	IA	Palomar College	CA
North Metro Technical Institute	GA	Pamlico Community College	NC
North Seattle Community College	WA	Panola College	TX
North Shore Community College	MA	Paradise Valley Community College	AZ
Northampton Community College	PA	Paris Junior College	TX
Northcentral Technical College	WI	Parkland College	IL
Northeast Community College	NE	Pasadena City College	CA
Northeast Iowa Community College	IA	Pasco-Hernando Community College	FL
Northeast State Technical Community College	TN	Passaic County Community College	NJ
Northeast Texas Community College	TX	Patrick Henry Community College	VA
Northeast Wisconsin Technical College	WI	Paul D Camp Community College	VA
Northeastern Junior College	CO	Pearl River Community College	MS
Northeastern Oklahoma Agricultural and		Pellissippi State Technical Community College	TN
Mechanical College	OK	Peninsula College	WA
Northeastern Technical College	SC	Pennsylvania Highlands Community College	PA
Northern Essex Community College	MA	Pennsylvania Institute of Technology	PA
Northern Maine Community College	ME	Pensacola Junior College	FL
Northern New Mexico Community College	NM	Phillips Community College of the	
Northern Oklahoma College	OK	University of Arkansas	AR
Northern Virginia Community College	VA	Phoenix College	AZ
Northland Community and Technical College	MN	Piedmont Community College	NC
Northland Pioneer College	AZ	Piedmont Technical College	SC
NorthWest Arkansas Community College	AR	Piedmont Virginia Community College	VA

College	State	College	State
Pierce College	WA	Santa Barbara City College	CA
Pierce College	CA	Santa Fe Community College	FL
Pikes Peak Community College	CO	Santa Fe Community College	NM
Polk Community College	FL	Santa Monica College	CA
Porterville College	CA	Santa Rosa Junior College	CA
Portland Community College	OR	Sauk Valley Community College	IL
Prairie State College	IL	Savannah Technical College	GA
Pratt Community College	KS	Schenectady County Community College	NY
Prince George's Community College	MD	Schoolcraft College	MI
Prince William Sound Community College	AK	Scottsdale Community College	AZ
Pueblo Community College	CO	Seattle Central Community College	WA
Pulaski Technical College	AR	Seminole Community College	FL
Purdue University North Central Campus	IN	Seward County Community College	KS
Queensborough Community College	NY	Shawnee Community College	IL
Quincy College	MA	Shelton State Community College	AL
Quinebaug Valley Community College	CT	Shoreline Community College	WA
Quinsigamond Community College	MA	Sinclair Community College	OH
Rainy River Community College	MN	Sisseton Wahpeton College	SD
Randolph Community College	NC	Skagit Valley College	WA
Ranger College	TX	Skyline College	CA
Ranken Technical College	MO	Snead State Community College	AL
Raritan Valley Community College	NJ	Somerset Community College	KY
Redlands Community College	OK	South Arkansas Community College	AR
Reedley College	CA	South Central College	MN
Rend Lake College	IL	South Florida Community College	FL
Renton Technical College	WA	South Louisiana Community College	LA
Rhodes College - Phoenix	AZ	South Mountain Community College	AZ
Richard Bland College	VA	South Piedmont Community College	NC
Richland College	TX	South Plains College	TX
Richland Community College	IL	South Puget Sound Community College	WA
Richmond Community College	NC	South Seattle Community College	WA
Ridgewater College	MN	South Suburban College	IL
Rio Hondo College	CA	South Texas College	TX
Rio Salado College	AZ	Southeast Arkansas College	AR
River Parishes Community College	LA	Southeast Community College	NE
Riverland Community College	MN	Southeast Community College	KY
Riverside Community College	CA	Southeast Missouri Hospital College of	
Roane State Community College	TN	Nursing and Health Services	MO
Roanoke-Chowan Community College	NC	Southeastern Community College	IA
Rochester Community and Technical College	MN	Southeastern Technical College	GA
Rock Valley College	IL	Southern Arkansas University Tech	AR
Rockingham Community College	NC	Southern Maine Community College	ME
Rockland Community College	NY	Southern State Community College	OH
Rogue Community College	OR	Southern University at Shreveport/Bossier City	LA
Rose State College	OK	Southern West Virginia Community and	
Rowan-Cabarrus Community College	NC	Technical College	WV
Saddleback College	CA	Southwest Georgia Technical College	GA
Saint Paul College	MN	Southwest Tennessee Community College	TN
Sampson Community College	NC	Southwest Texas Junior College	TX
San Antonio College	TX	Southwest Wisconsin Technical College	WI
San Diego City College	CA	Southwestern College	CA
San Diego Miramar College	CA	Southwestern Community College	NC
San Jacinto College District	TX	Southwestern Community College	IA
San Joaquin Delta College	CA	Southwestern Michigan College	MI
San Juan College	NM	Southwestern Oregon Community College	OR
Santa Ana College	CA	Sowela Technical Community College	LA

College	State	College	State
Spokane Community College	WA	University of Hawai'i Kapi'olani Community College	HI
Spokane Falls Community College	WA	University of Hawai'i-Hawai'i Community College	HI
Spoon River College	IL	University of Hawai'i-Honolulu Community College	HI
St Augustine College	IL	University of Hawai'i-Maui Community College	HI
St Catharine College	KY	University of Hawai'i-Windward Community College	HI
St Charles Community College	MO	University of Montana-Helena College of Technology	MT
St Clair County Community College	MI	University of Northwestern Ohio	OH
St Cloud Technical College	MN	Valdosta Technical College	GA
St Elizabeth College of Nursing	NY	Valencia Community College	FL
St Johns River Community College	FL	Valley Forge Military College	PA
St Louis Community College	MO	Ventura College	CA
St Petersburg College	FL	Vermillion Community College	MN
St Philip's College	TX	Vernon Regional Junior College	TX
Stanly Community College	NC	Victor Valley College	CA
Stark State College of Technology	OH	Victoria College	TX
State Fair Community College	MO	Villa Maria College of Buffalo	NY
Suffolk County Community College	NY	Virginia Highlands Community College	VA
Sullivan County Community College	NY	Virginia Western Community College	VA
SUNY Canton	NY	Volunteer State Community College	TN
Surry Community College	NC	Walla Walla Community College	WA
Sussex County Community College	NJ	Wallace Community College	AL
Tacoma Community College	WA	Wallace State Community College	AL
Taft College	CA	Walters State Community College	TN
Tallahassee Community College	FL	Warren County Community College	NJ
Tarrant County College District	TX	Washington County Community College	ME
Technical College of the Lowcountry	SC	Washington State Community College	OH
Temple College	TX	Washtenaw Community College	MI
Terra State Community College	OH	Waubonsee Community College	IL
Texas State Technical College-Harlingen	TX	Waukesha County Technical College	WI
Texas State Technical College-Marshall	TX	Waycross College	GA
Texas State Technical College-Waco	TX	Wayne Community College	NC
Texas State Technical College-West Texas	TX	Wayne County Community College District	MI
The Art Institute of Dallas	TX	Wenatchee Valley College	WA
The Metropolitan Community Colleges	MO	Wentworth Military Academy and Junior College	MO
The Urban College of Boston	MA	West Central Technical College Carrollton Campus	GA
Thomas Nelson Community College	VA	West Georgia Technical College	GA
Three Rivers Community College	CT	West Hills Community College	CA
Three Rivers Community College	MO	West Shore Community College	MI
Tidewater Community College	VA	Westchester Community College	NY
Tillamook Bay Community College	OR	Western Dakota Technical Institute	SD
TransPacific Hawaii College	HI	Western Iowa Tech Community College	IA
Treasure Valley Community College	OR	Western Nebraska Community College Area	NE
Tri-County Community College	NC	Western Nevada Community College	NV
Trident Technical College	SC	Western Oklahoma State College	OK
Trinity Valley Community College	TX	Western Piedmont Community College	NC
Triton College	IL	Western Texas College	TX
Trocaire College	NY	Western Wisconsin Technical College	WI
Truckee Meadows Community College	NV	Western Wyoming Community College	WY
Truman College	IL	Westmoreland County Community College	PA
Tulsa Community College	OK	Wharton County Junior College	TX
Tunxis Community College	CT	Wilbur Wright College	IL
Tyler Junior College	TX	Wilkes Community College	NC
University of Arkansas Community College-Morrilton	AR	Williamsburg Technical College	SC
University of Arkansas-Fort Smith	AR	Williston State College	ND
Union County College	NJ	Wilson Technical Community College	NC
University of Cincinnati-Raymond Walters College	OH	Wisconsin Indianhead Technical College	WI

College	State
Wor-Wic Community College	MD
Yakima Valley Community College	WA
York County Community College	ME
York Technical College	SC
Zane State College	OH

Appendix C:
American Association of Community Colleges 2004 Ad Hoc Task Force on Homeland Security

David Buettner, Fox Valley Technical College (WI)

George Coxey, Owens Community College (OH)

Vernon Crawley, Moraine Valley Community College (IL)

Larry Devane, Redlands Community College (OK)

Mary Ellen Duncan (2004 Co-Chair), Howard Community College (MD)

Doug Feil, Kirkwood Community College (IA)

R. Thomas Flynn, Monroe Community College (NY)

Margaret Forde, Houston Community College System-Northeast College (TX)

Herlinda Glasscock, Dallas County Community College District, North Lake College (TX)

Pat Keir, San Diego Miramar College (CA)

Carl Kuttler, St. Petersburg College (FL)

Antonio Perez (2004–2005 Co-Chair), Borough of Manhattan Community College (NY)

Don Snyder, Lehigh Carbon Community College (PA)

Mary Spangler (2005 Co-Chair), Oakland Community College (MI)

Gwen Stephenson, Hillsborough Community College (FL)

Robert Templin, Northern Virginia Community College (VA)

Frank Toda, Columbia Gorge Community College (OR)

Art Tyler, Los Angeles City College (CA)

Steve Wall, Pierce College (WA)

Frances White, Skyline College (CA)

Tony Zeiss, Central Piedmont Community College (NC)